The Lost Cott
of Central Texas

Jack Howell

i

John R. (Jack) Howell has enjoyed a life-long interest in antique mechanical equipment. He and his wife, Susan Conway, have traveled extensively and have visited many engineering and technical sites around the world. He is a member of the US National Academy of Engineering, a Foreign Member of the Russian Academy of Science, and a Life Fellow in the American Society of Mechanical Engineers. He recently retired from teaching in Mechanical Engineering at The University of Texas-Austin, but remains active in research.

Table of Contents

Preface

Central Texas was a major cotton producer until well into the Depression. Although cotton production continues at about a constant level across the State, it has dwindled as a part of the economy of Central Texas. The infrastructure that supported Central Texas cotton production included the cotton gins required to remove the seed and trash from picked cotton, the cotton presses needed to compress the picked cotton into bales suitable for shipping, cotton seed mills for extracting cottonseed oil and providing seed for replanting, and the commercial enterprise necessary to market, finance and coordinate all of this. Cotton was a large part of the pre-Depression economy, and many Central Texas communities were built around it.

This book concentrates on the cotton gins themselves (with a few asides), and what has become of them as cotton production in Central Texas has declined.

Operating a gin was always perilous business. The year-to-year variations in weather and market price made the annual business outlook chancy. Gin operation was compressed into a few months as the crop came in, and the capital equipment in the gin sat idle for much of the year. Gin fires were extremely common (and are referred to often in the individual gin histories in succeeding pages), and if a gin was on the edge of profitability, rebuilding after a fire might not make economic sense.

In the early twentieth century, almost every village had a cotton gin, and larger towns often had two or more to service the local production of hand-picked cotton. During the Depression years, low cotton prices coupled with the relatively small size of most cotton farms in the area (plus the continuing fight with the boll weevil) caused a rapid decline in cotton production in Central Texas. The loss of production caused many gins to close, and their skeletons remain a part of the rural Texas landscape.

The abandoned gins often inhabit plots of land of low present value; otherwise, they are subject to being demolished or have already been demolished to make way for new development. A few abandoned gins remain in towns and cities where their forlorn state is tolerated in the hope of refurbishment into new commercial or community uses, and some have been converted to restaurants, wineries, or community dance halls or music venues. However, relentless pressure for development means that the abandoned gins continue to disappear. Unless the gin buildings are being recycled for other uses, communities seem to view them as eyesores and reminders of what may be now viewed as a painful past, and tend to ignore their presence.

As the gins are lost, they can no longer serve as reminders of an important chapter of a vibrant Central Texas history, and it is hoped that the photographs in this book will help to keep them alive at least in our memories.

The Lost Cotton Gins
of Central Texas

The Cotton Gin

Every schoolchild has heard the story of Eli Whitney and his invention of the cotton gin. The introduction of the gin in 1793 changed the American economy. Quite simply, the gin provided mechanical removal of the entrained and very difficult to remove cotton seed from the desirable cotton fibers, allowing fast and efficient production of high quality cotton. The gin allowed the foundation of a cotton-based system of agriculture, probably prolonged the system of slavery, and spurred widespread cotton production in the southern US.

Model of Whitney's Cotton Gin
(courtesy Smithsonian Museum of American History)

The gin (a shortening of the word *engine*) now seems a simple device. It is made up of rotating blades with teeth (*saws*) that protrude through narrow slots into a box loaded with unprocessed fibers and their tenacious seed. The blades grab the fibers, and pull them through the blade slots, leaving behind the many cotton seeds, which are too large to pass through the slots.

Early gins on plantations were powered by individual labor and later by mules or horses. As gins grew larger and more centralized, power was provided by steam engines, waterpower, diesel engines, and most recently by electric motors.

Cotton Production in Texas

Following early explosive growth in cotton production in Texas, the total production of cotton in Texas has increased slowly over the past hundred years, with a dip in production during the years of the Great Depression and a generally increasing trend (with large year-to-year fluctuations due to market and weather conditions) from about 1962 to the present. The acreage devoted to cotton in Texas has decreased from over 18 million acres in the mid-1920s to roughly 5 to 7 million acres since 1950. Greatly increased productivity has allowed increasing production despite decreasing acreage devoted to the crop, and cotton remains the chief cash crop in Texas. Pounds of cotton per harvested acre in a good year seldom exceeded 200 until the 1950s, when the introduction of mechanized cotton picking machinery caused yields to usually exceed 300 pounds per acre, and occasionally reach 500. These statistics also reflect a shift in production to large operations, and away from the 100-acre share-croppers and small farms found in central Texas prior to the Depression.

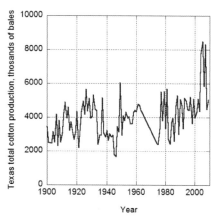

Total Texas cotton production in bales/year from 1901-2009
(Source, USDA Agricultural Statistics Service and Texas Department of Agriculture Statistics Service. Figures are for 500 pound bales through 1952 and 480 pound bales thereafter.)

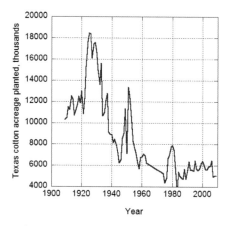

Total Texas cotton acreage planted from 1909-2009
(Source, USDA Agricultural Statistics Service and Texas Department of Agriculture Statistics Service)

Cotton in Central Texas

The importance of cotton in Central Texas dates back to Stephen F. Austin's initiative to bring in cotton farmers to settle his land grant, beginning in 1822. The Mexican government was opposed to slavery, so large cotton plantations weren't initially economical, as they depended heavily on slave labor. Farmers and cotton growers did move in to settle relatively small plots that could be handled by a single family, and the rate of settlement mushroomed after Texas independence. Many of the settlers in this period were recent immigrants looking for a new start. Czechs, Wendish, Germans, Swedes, and others tended to begin small cotton farms of the size conveniently planted and cared for by a family with a mule or horse, usually about 100 acres. Following Texas independence, large cotton plantations based on slave labor did begin to appear in the Brazos River bottoms, but small farms remained the norm in the blackland and upland prairies.

Cotton production boomed in all of Texas throughout the years from the establishment of Austin's grant until the Depression. Small farms were profitable in years of average to good weather, and a family was able to grow sufficient food to maintain themselves and perhaps a surplus of farm products to sell, while income from the cotton crop provided the cash to buy seed for the next year's planting, investment in new equipment, a little to put aside to prepare for the next bad year, and possibly a few pleasures as well. In bad years, which were common, the weather could cause a partial or total loss of the cotton crop, and a very hard year to follow. Cotton farming was a gambler's game.

Given the small farms, the terrible roads, and the reliance on horses, oxen and mules for transport, small cotton gins sprang up in nearly every community to serve the local area. In 1914, there were over 4600 gins operating in Texas. Because the gins were in operation for only a few months of the year, they were often poorly and cheaply constructed, but were able to adequately gin hand-picked cotton and make it suitable to market and ship.

Cotton acreage in Texas reached an all-time high in 1925 and 1926, when over 18 million acres were devoted to cotton. In 1927, cotton sold in Texas for an average price of over 20 cents per pound. By the depression year of 1930 the price was under 10 cents, and in 1931, went to 5.6 cents. Many cotton farmers and sharecroppers were unable to stay afloat at these market prices during the Depression, and this was especially the case for the labor-intensive small farms in Central Texas.

The boll weevil
(Courtesy USDA Agricultural Research Service)

By the time the price rose again in the war years after 1941 to over 15 cents a pound, planted cotton acreage in Texas had fallen below 8.2 million.

The number of gins operating in Texas followed the drop in cotton production, and by 1940 had dropped to under 3000.

Following World War II, cotton prices and production made a resurgence; however, production had already begun to shift to the High Plains and the Texas Panhandle. The advent of the mechanical cotton picker reduced labor costs so that large cotton farms could be more economically planted, and land there was available in large blocks. In addition, the boll weevil had not yet invaded the new region (although it soon would), but it had devastated cotton production in Central Texas. Newer cotton gins also took advantage of the economies of scale and ease of transportation now available with improved roads, tractors, and trucks, and very large gins appeared in the Panhandle. The smaller gins common in Central Texas were faced with two problems; a declining customer base, and the need to replace ginning machinery with modern equipment that could remove the increased level of trash that was found in machine-pulled cotton. Many older and smaller gins could not compete, and were simply abandoned in place.

Small farm-based communities in Central Texas also felt the fallout from this shift in economics. Almost every such town had at least one gin, and possibly a seed mill, cotton press, cotton market, or rail shipping center. The loss of this segment of the local economy along with the decreased farm income from the loss of cotton sales led to the many declining, ghost- or near ghost-towns that can be found on a trip on any back-country road through Central Texas. Often, the entire cotton infrastructure that once graced these towns is completely gone. The names may remain, such as Payton Gin Road in Austin, and the many other such "Gin Roads" throughout the area. Near the old Swedish-immigrant farming community of New Sweden, near Austin, is Sweden Gin road; such names are always worth a search by a gin hunter, and indeed this one did lead the author to find an abandoned and overgrown gin building hidden beside the road.

In contrast to the statewide increase in production, Central Texas has shown a continuing decline. For example, production decreased In Fayette County to fewer than 500 bales per year in 1973, and the USDA quit tracking production after 1974. Nearby Bastrop County has maintained a constant but low production of a few hundred bales per year, not exceeding 1000 bales since 1970. This fall in production is typical of the counties in the Central Texas region. The boll weevil has now been almost completely eradicated, but it is too late to reverse the changes in the Central Texas economy and bring cotton back as the dominating factor it once was.

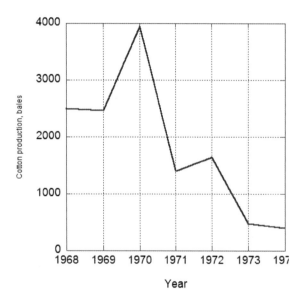

Bales of Cotton Produced in Fayette County, Texas by Year
(USDA Agricultural Statistics Service and Texas Department of Agriculture Statistics Service)

Armed with an understanding of why cotton gins are rapidly disappearing from Central Texas, the remainder of this book reports on journeys through Central Texas, to preserve at least photographically what is left of an important part of Texas history. The gins that are shown are from roughly a two-county tier around Travis County shown in the map, although some exceptions exist. No claim is made that all abandoned gins in the region have been found, as there is no way to pinpoint their existence except through talking with local people familiar with the area and driving the back roads, and there are many miles of such roads in Central Texas!

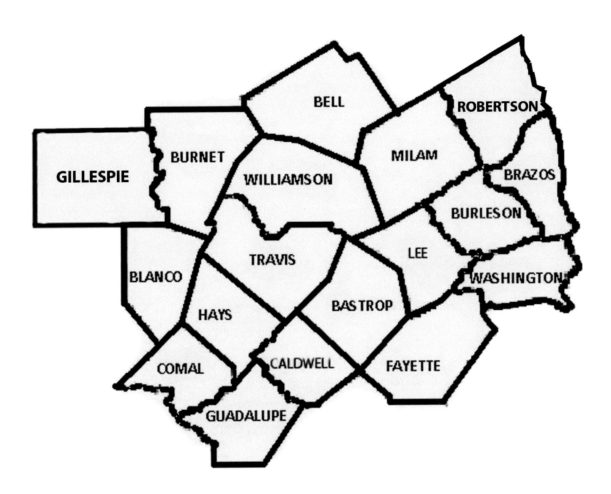

Central Texas Counties covered in this book.

The Ammannsville Mill and Gin

The Ammannsville gin is located on Farm Road 1383 (off Hwy 77) in Fayette County. It is about 9 miles southeast of La Grange, 28 miles northwest of Columbus. The town is named after Andrew Ammann, who arrived on March 12, 1870. Various spellings for the town name exist on contemporary maps.

FAYETTE COUNTY

LaGrange

Ammannsville

1383

77

Ammannsville had two gins during its heyday. The *Weimar Mercury* of January 24 and 31, 1889 reported from Ammannsville that "Two gins and mills are next in order. One is owned by Mr. Theophil Heller, one of the wealthiest men in Fayette County, and the other by Messrs. Mewes and Koenig. The former has been elected Squire recently, and is an energetic young man who is not afraid of anybody, metes out justice without fear and partiality."

Marie L. Albrecht and
Joseph J. (J.J.) Munke, mill owners
(Courtesy of Jon Todd Koenig)

and passed through a series of owners, fires, and rebuildings. The Heller gin was demolished and rebuilt with modern machinery in 1879; was destroyed by fire and again rebuilt in 1888. It burned a final time, and the land was then sold.

According to "A History of Ammannsville (1870-1935)" published in the *Mercury* in 1935, the gin referred to was originally built in 1877 by Theophil Heller, Sr.,

The second gin was erected by Mr. Joseph J. Barta on a second site a few years later with new machinery. It is the one pictured here. It operated until 1954, when it proved uneconomical to completely modify the gin stands to handle the "pulled" cotton that was becoming prevalent in this area of Texas, as cotton picking moved from manual picking by field hands and on to mechanical cotton strippers, which carried much waste along with the cotton to be ginned. As with any gin, a junk pile

of discarded and unused parts fills a portion of the lot.

This is one of the few abandoned gins, along with the Theon gin, that retains its ginning equipment.

12

Bartlett Gins and Oil Press

Bartlett remains a busy town, although cotton has become a minor segment of the businesses both in town and along the former Missouri-Kansas-Texas (Katy, now part of the Union Pacific) railroad tracks.

Bartlett Gin #1

This gin is located beside State Route 95 in Bartlett.

Bartlett Gin #2

Right: Cotton Seed Bin

Bartlett Oil Mill

Oil mills were used to produce cottonseed oil from the seeds extracted during the ginning process. The first bottled cottonseed oil appeared in 1892. Modern mills can produce about 190 pounds of oil from the 790 pounds of seed extracted per bale of ginned cotton. Because the oil is trans-fat free, it has seen resurgence in production because of present-day dietary concerns.

Unfortunately for Bartlett, the fractured stack standing alone beside the old Katy tracks is all that remains of the Bartlett oil mill. The original mill nearly burned in early 1905 when the nearby American Round Bale Gin burned, and did burn sometime in late 1905. A replacement was built shortly thereafter, and was in operation by late 1906. It has now disappeared.

Belton Co-op Gin

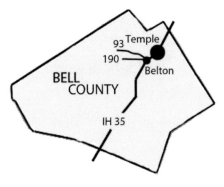

The handsome brick Belton Farmers Co-op Gin backs up to Nolan Creek. The Co-op building is at 219 South East Avenue, and is listed in the National Register of Historic Places. It is contained in the designated Belton Commercial Historic District.

This is another gin that cries out for restoration and re-use. Belton is struggling to find the formula that will bring it back. The Belton City Council has commissioned *a Historic Preservation Action Plan* as well as a study of *Design Guidelines for Historic Belton, Texas* with a view to retaining and upgrading the many historic residences and structures within the city limits. Plans to convert the gin buildings into a restaurant and events center are on hold. At last check, a construction company planned to remodel the façade and move into the building.

Beyersville Gins

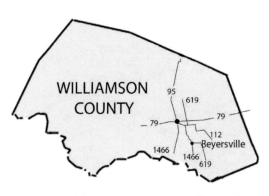

One 1932-era Beyersville gin is tucked just east of FM 619 on County Road 451 in southeastern Williamson County. It is now partially converted to a car and truck repair center. Aside from the fact that Gustav Beyers established the Post Office in his name in 1893 in a village formerly known as Dacus Crossing, little more of the town history is known.

On the west side of FM 619 is another lost gin. According to Ralph Bachmeyer, grandson of the builder/owner, this gin was originally powered by an oil-fired steam engine with a 16 foot diameter flywheel which turned slowly enough that boys used to hang on as it revolved (no OSHA in those days). The gin burned at least once when crude oil overflowed while being transferred into an overhead fuel tank, and caught fire. The gin was immediately rebuilt. The new building was damaged by a 1962 tornado, and was rebuilt/repaired at that time reducing its original height to its present 16 feet. The overgrown control panel for an attached diesel engine can be seen, below right.

Beyersville surely retains the title of most abandoned gins per capita.

Blumenthal Engine

All that remains of an old gin in Blumenthal is a rusted but quite impressive small Brownell steam engine and boiler.

Blumenthal is between Stonewall and Fredericksburg on SH 290. The engine lies to the North of the highway and is between the highway and the Pedernales River, which dips toward the highway at that point. The original gin (and engine) was in the town, and the remaining town

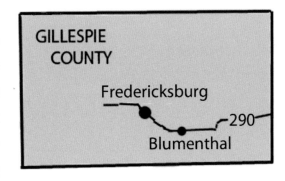

buildings now make up the Blumenthal B&B. The engine sits just west of the building complex.

The steam engine and boiler were products of The Brownell Company of Dayton, Ohio, which sold small steam engines for use in sawmills, paper mills, and cotton gins. The firm opened business in 1865, and by 1909, had a capacity of producing 2500 boilers and 500 engines. It was still in business in 1939, but is now gone from the Dayton scene, although some of the original factory buildings remain.

Farmers Brazos Gin Company

This gin and its adjacent oil mill have been integrated into storage space on a farm; they are located on Reistino Gin Road, which parallels the Union Pacific tracks between Mooring and Mumford just west of SH 50 in Robertson County. Reistino Gin Road can be entered from the North via Watts Road from SH 50, or via Reistino Road itself from SH 50 from the South, where it crosses the UP tracks.

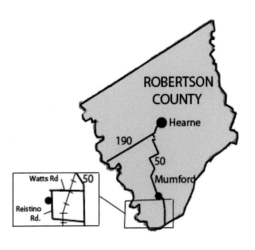

Burton

Burton lies about halfway between Austin and Houston just north of US 290, so it is somewhat outside the rough boundary of the region otherwise considered in this book. However, no discussion of abandoned Texas gins would be complete without

WASHINGTON COUNTY
290
Burton

mention of Burton (pop.≈ 350) and its annual Cotton Gin Festival

The Burton Farmers Gin, built in 1914, operated until 1974. Since 1994, it has only operated on Festival weekends. The Smithsonian deems it "the oldest operating cotton gin in America". It is also designated a National Historic Engineering Landmark by the American Society of Mechanical Engineers; listed on the National Register of Historic Places and is designated a Texas Historic Landmark by the Texas Historical Commission. In 1987, local preservationists established *Operation Restoration* to save the gin, and were successful. Tours of the gin are given twice daily, Tuesday through Saturday.

The gin was originally powered by a wood-fired (later coal fired) steam engine, but now sports the "Lady B," a 125 horsepower 1925 Bessemer Type IV diesel oil engine, which powered the gin between 1925 and 1963. From 1963 until closure in 1974, a 125 HP Allis Chalmers electric motor was used. The restored "Lady B" is claimed to be the largest internal combustion engine of its vintage still operating in America.

In 1974, only 7 bales of cotton were ginned, and commercial operation ended that year.

The Burton Cotton Gin Festival, usually held in April, is an excellent slice of Texana, and below are some photos from the tractor show, parade and the midway of the festival in 2010.

**Texas Cotton Gin Museum
(Official Cotton Gin Museum of
Texas)**

P.O. Box 98
Burton, TX 77835
979-289-3378
979-289-5210
www.cottonginmuseum.org

Coupland Gin

Coupland lies just across the northeastern Travis County line in Williamson County, just East of SH 95. The original Taylor, Bastrop and Houston Railway tracks (now part of the Union Pacific) divide the gin from the town proper. The main street of Coupland parallels the tracks as it should in all good railroad towns.

Coupland is home to the Coupland Inn, famous for chicken-fried steaks (and it also was host to the author's wedding rehearsal dinner). The adjacent dance hall is a weekend gathering spot for the area. The gin itself clearly had prosperous days, but is now abandoned.

Dime Box Gin

The villages of Dime Box and Old Dime Box are a part of Texas lore. The name is said to come from the practice of leaving a dime in a box at Brown's Mill (now Old Dime Box) to assure getting a letter delivered to nearby Giddings. A Federal Post Office opened in 1877 (and closed in 1893). The Southern Pacific (now part of the Union Pacific) ran tracks about 3 miles to the southeast of Old Dime Box in 1913,

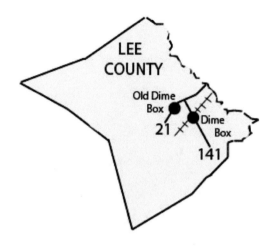

and many of the citizens moved to the new site. Both towns survive. They are about 15 miles north of Giddings on SH 21 in Lee County.

Elgin Oil Press and Gin

Elgin was blessed with having two railroads choose it as a waypoint. The first was the East-West oriented Houston and Texas Central which built through the area in 1871. This line became part of the Union Pacific after various mergers and name changes. The UP sold the line from Giddings through LaGrange to Llano to the City of Austin, and the freight operation is now run by the Austin Western Railroad under contract to the present right-of-way owners, Capital Metropolitan Transportation Authority (Cap Metro) of Austin. The East-West line was followed in 1886 by a North-South branch line, the Taylor, Elgin and Bastrop. The latter line was bought by the Missouri-Kansas-Texas (M-K-T or "Katy") line the same year, and now is also part of the Union Pacific. Eight passenger trains per day visited Elgin in the heyday of railroading, and the connections available by rail made Elgin a major agricultural shipping center during the boom cotton years.

The Elgin Gin

In the 1940-50 period, Elgin boasted 5 operating cotton gins. Most have disappeared. One interesting relic remains on Second Street, well south of the town center and quite near the town water tower.

The Elgin Oil Mill

Although cottonseed oil has made a resurgence in the market for edible vegetable oils because it is free of trans-fats and is cheap compared with most other vegetable oils, it has some negative factors as well. It contains high levels of omega-6 fatty acids, has the potential for high levels of pesticide, and may have the presence of the natural toxin gossypol, which must be removed by processing. Its expanded market has kept the Elgin Oil Mill in business since its organization in 1906, and it now produces about 250,000 gallons of cottonseed oil per year.

The mill uses the expeller method of oil extraction rather than the more common solvent extraction method. It is said to be one of four in Texas and 12 in the US still using this method. A promising market has opened for conversion of cottonseed oil into biodiesel, and some of the Elgin mill's output went to manufacture Willie Nelson's product, Biowillie.

After oil extraction, the pressed seeds still retain a high level of protein and can be used as a cattle feed supplement or a crop fertilizer. This trackside building in Elgin probably once served as a car loading and storage area for seed meal.

Elroy Gin

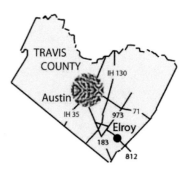

Elroy is a small town at the intersection of FM 812 and Elroy Road, to the East of the IH 130 bypass around Austin. It has had several names in the past, including Driskill, Dutch Waterhole, and Hume. The present name came about in 1892, when a Post Office designation was sought, and, according to the *Handbook of Texas On Line*, the name submitted was an anagram of the name Leroy, son of a local storeowner. Elroy has gained recognition as the present home of *Wild Bubba's*

Wild Game Grill, which serves fried coyote tail (hot dogs in bread) as well as antelope, kangaroo, yak, and black bear burgers. It is also the future home of a Formula One race track, which will undoubtedly change its present sleepy status when it hosts the 2012 Grand Prix.

The Elroy Gin lies about 100 yards to the South of FM 812, across the road from *Wild Bubba's*. All the ginning equipment has been removed. The Gin was built in 1916 as the Swedish Farmer's Gin, and became the Elroy Farmer's Gin in 1921. It converted to the Elroy Cooperative Gin 1950.

Extraterrestrials and Texas Cotton

Texas cotton and cotton gins appear to have a particular fascination for extraterrestrials and UFOs, a fact recorded as long ago as late in the 19th Century. Here are two examples:

Between Dublin and Stephenville, Erath County:

"A Meteor Explodes in the City—An Eye Witness Describes the Scene to a Progress Reporter—Scared.

Quite a little excitement was created last Saturday night by the bursting of what is supposed by those who were present to have been a meteor, near Wasson & Miller's gin. Quite a number witnessed the explosion and nearly everyone in that portion of the city heard the report emanating [sic] therefrom, which is said to have sounded somewhat like the report of a bomb-shell. Our informant (who, though a little nervous at times, is a gentleman who usually tells the truth, but did not give us this statement with a view to its publication) says he observed the meteor when it was more than three hundred feet in the air, before bursting, and that it bore a striking resemblance to a bale of cotton suspended in the air after having been saturated in kerosene oil and ignited, except that it created a much brighter light, almost dazzling those who percieved [sic] it. The gentleman in question seems to have been so badly frightened that it was utterly impossible to obtain an accurate account of the dimensions and general appearance of this rare phenomenon, but we are convinced from his statements that his position at the time must have been very embarrassing and that very little time was spent in scientific investigations. However, on the following morning he returned to the scene so hastily left the previous night, to find the weeds, grass, bushes and vegetation of every description for many yards around the scene of the explosion burned to a crisp, also discovering a number of peculiar stones and pieces of metal, all of a leaden color, presenting much the appearance of the lava thrown out by volcanic eruptions. He also picked up some small fragments of manuscript and a scrap, supposed to be part of a newspaper, but the language in both was

40

entirely foreign to him, and, in fact, no one has yet been found who has ever seen such a language before, hence no information could be gained from their examination. At this juncture your reporter requested that he be shown these wonderful fragments of such a miraculous whole, but the narrator had worked himself up to such a pitch of excitement that it was impossible to get him to grasp the significance of our request, and were compelled to leave him a victim to his own bewildered fancy and to ruminate the seemingly miraculous story he had just related. Thus was a repotorial [sic] zealot denied the boon of seeing fragments of the most remarkable substance ever known to explode near Wasson & Miller's gin.

P.S. Since the above was put in type we learn that our reporter was given the above information by a contributor to the Dublin Telephone, but the information came too late to prevent its insertion in this paper."

Dublin Progress, June 20, 1891

Aurora, Texas

Near Aurora is a historical marker for the Aurora Cemetery that reads, in part, "...This site is also well-known because of the legend that a spaceship crashed nearby in 1897 and the pilot, killed in the crash, was buried here."

"About 6 o'clock this morning the early risers of Aurora were astonished at the sudden appearance of the airship which has been sailing around the country.

It was traveling due north and much nearer the earth than before. Evidently some of the machinery was out of order, for it was making a speed of only ten or twelve miles an hour, and gradually settling toward the earth. It sailed over the public square and when it reached the north part of town it collided with the tower of Judge Proctor's windmill and went into pieces with a terrific explosion, scattering debris over several acres of ground, wrecking the windmill and water tank and destroying the judge's flower garden. The pilot of the ship is supposed to have been the only one aboard and, while his remains were badly disfigured, enough of the original has been picked up to show that he was not an inhabitant of this world.

Mr. T.J. Weems, the U.S. Army Signal Service officer at this place and an authority on astronomy gives it as his opinion that the pilot was a native of the planet Mars. Papers found on his person -- evidently the records of his travels -- are written in some unknown hieroglyphics and cannot be deciphered. This ship was too badly wrecked to form any conclusion as to its construction or motive power. It was built of an unknown metal, resembling somewhat a mixture of aluminum and silver, and it must have weighed several tons. The town is today full of people who are viewing the wreckage and gathering specimens of strange metal from the debris. The pilot's funeral will take place tomorrow."
Dallas Morning News, April 19, 1897.

Although it isn't clear that Judge Proctor's windmill was adjacent to a cotton field, it seems probable given the location and date. The motives of the early ETs in checking out Texas cotton are unclear, but in addition to an undecipherable written language, they do seem to have had extremely poor piloting skills.

As recently as January 2008, a UFO was again sighted near Stephenville, and in October, 2008, a professional photographer was taking pictures of cotton gins (!!) near Lubbock, and later found a UFO in one of the frames. (See: http://www.nationalufocenter.com/artman/publish/article_253.php).

Watch the skies!

Fentress Gin

Fentress was established through the confluence of a Cumberland Presbyterian church established in 1869 and a horse-powered cotton gin built in the vicinity about 1870. The gin enterprise was moved to the San Marcos riverfront and converted to waterpower in 1879; it was operated by descendents of the founders, Cullen R. Smith and Joseph D. Smith, until it closed in 1968.

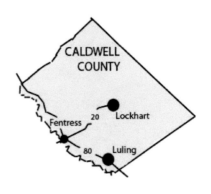

According to *The Handbook of Texas On Line,* Josh Merritt and his partner C. E. Tolhurst created a Fentress resort in 1915 that offered bathhouses, a water slide, and screened tents with wooden floors.

Merritt and Tolhorst later sold the resort. The new owners added a maple-floored skating rink, and permitted dancing on alternating nights. This caused some consternation among devout church members in surrounding communities. In 1918 the six-year-old Fentress water tower collapsed onto the town's only bank and the cashier was forced to dash into the vault to save his life. This was viewed by some as a divine judgment on dancing.

After a period of growth fueled by oilfield activity, a long decline began for the village. Even the Fentress Hog Farm, which once supplied successive title holders to Aquarena Springs of *Ralph, The World-Famous Diving Pig*, no longer exists.

Florence Gin

Florence is on State Highway 195, 17 miles northwest of Georgetown. The gin is about a block to the west of SH 195 on Farm Road 970. The gin was built in 1903, and was at one time converted to an antique store, but when visited in 2010 it was for sale.

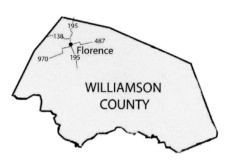

The Florence gin is one of the few lying to the west of IH 35 in Central Texas. The land in much of the Texas Hill Country in that area is not well suited to cotton, although production did occur early in the twentieth century and many small towns had gins. These have mostly disappeared.

Fredericksburg

Alas, Fredericksburg embodies all of the reasons this book seems necessary. In the summer of 2009, the annual peach-buying and shop-hopping trip to Fredericksburg with my wife resulted in finding a recently defunct gin along the East side of SH 87

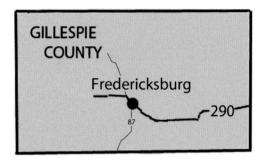

(Washington Street) between Walnut and Hale. Because this was not a gin-searching sojourn, my camera was not along. I resolved to return, and in early November, 2010, I checked the satellite maps for the exact location, and the gin was there. On November 17, 2010, I headed for Fredericksburg, photographing the steam engine at Blumenthal and the feed mill/gin in Johnson City along the way. When I arrived at Fredericksburg, here is what I found at the site:

Missed by about a week! The bulldozer tracks and ruts are still easily visible. Another gin lost to progress.

 Not too far away, on Park Street, is an old peanut processing and peanut oil plant, now abandoned. The beautiful old buildings almost made the trip worthwhile. Not a cotton gin? No, but indeed a disappearing part of the Central Texas agricultural past.

Galle Gin

Galle (pron. "Golley") is the perfect example of roadside gin serendipity. After checking an abandoned gin in Geronimo, which turned out to have been so modified into an antique shop that it didn't seem worth photographing, I set off for Staples, Texas, which I knew had a photogenic gin but which I had missed on previous trips into the area. I chose to take FM 1339 from just north of Geronimo to Staples, and on the way passed through Galle, which has a few houses along the road and the surprise of the abandoned gin shown in these pictures. The property was festooned with *No Trespassing* and *For Sale* signs; I neither trespassed nor bought, but took the photographs below. A few miles further along the road was a cotton field in full bloom.

Gin Manufacturers

Early gins were built on individual farms and plantations, and were powered by hand, mules or horses. As more efficient gins were invented, manufactured gins became common, and small companies sprung up across the South to meet the need for gin equipment. Such gins were more expensive, but had higher capacity, and farmers banded together to form cooperative gins.

Robert S. Munger invented an integrated gin system in Mexia in 1883 that greatly reduced the manpower previously required to move cotton among the various operations in the gin. The Munger Improved Cotton Machine Manufacturing Company began to manufacture gin equipment in 1884 in the Deep Ellum region of Dallas. Munger merged his company with several smaller manufacturers to form the Continental Gin Company in 1899. The Dallas gin plant has now been converted into the Continental Loft Apartments.

When the Munger system introduced integrated ginning in the late 19th century, a race began to consolidate the smaller gin manufacturers. This led to the formation of three major competitors; the Continental Gin Company (1899), the Lummus Cotton Gin Company (1910), and the Murray Gin Company (1912) which succeeded the E. Van Winkle Gin and Machine Works (1889-1912). Signs for each of these gin equipment providers can be seen on one or more of the gin photographs shown in this book.

Manufacture of gin machinery was one of the few areas of mechanical equipment manufacture that was not dominated by industry in the North, and it provided a strong manufacturing base for the Southern states through the late 19th and early 20th centuries. Recently, a drop in market demand has caused even more consolidation of the US gin manufacturers. Murray and Continental merged in 1986 to form the Continental Eagle Corporation, and Lummus completed the agglomeration by merging with Continental Eagle in 2010 to form United Ginning.

Gruene

The original cotton gin in Gruene was built shortly after 1879 on the site of a grist mill that used the Guadalupe River for power. It was later converted to steam. The gin burned in 1922; only the boiler room remains, and it's now part of the *Gristmill River Restaurant and Bar*. A newer electrically-powered gin was built nearby, and operated until 1925, when the boll weevil and soil depletion destroyed local cotton productivity; the building is now converted into the *Adobe Verde* restaurant.

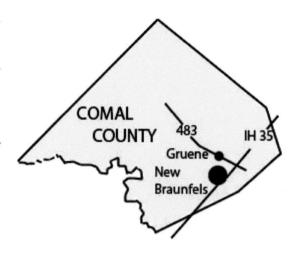

Gristmill River Restaurant, built around the old Gruene gin boiler room

The boiler room at the Gristmill, all that remains of the original gin and mill, now built into the restaurant

The Adobe Verde restaurant, now occupying the site of the "new" gin at Gruene.

Hare Gin

According to the Handbook of Texas On Line, local folklore maintains that early settler William Caesar, who bought land in the area in the 1880s, said that Hare was named for the abundant cottontails in the vicinity. Subscribers to this theory claim that the community was also known by the nickname "Fuzzy." Other sources think the community was named after a pioneer family whose surname was Hare.

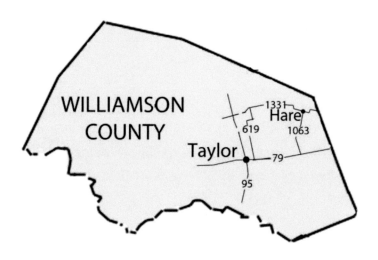

Hare has an abandoned co-op gin. This photograph was taken in June, 2006. On returning about four years later, the gin was no longer operating, and was being converted to an undetermined use. There is also what appears to be a much older gin that remains in downtown Hare. It's a prime example of a gin that will probably be torn down if property values increase to the point where the land it occupies makes demolition worthwhile.

Hoxie Gin

Hoxie is at the confluence of County Roads 417 and 418 in Williamson County, a few miles south of Granger Lake. It now exists as a village mostly in imagination, but has a glorious past. John R. Hoxie was a former mayor of Chicago and a railroad magnate who established a magnificent estate called Hoxie House on 9000 acres of land, where he raised horses and cattle. He purchased the land in 1878 from the heirs of Dr. Asa Hoxie, a veteran of the Texan and the Mexican Wars, and an army surgeon under General Sam Houston. The house was completed in 1882, and supposedly the City of Austin

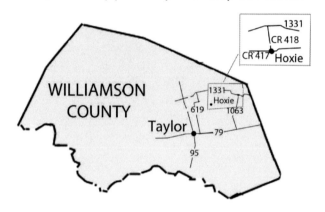

could be seen from the upper floors on a clear day. John died in November, 1896. The estate was split into small farms in 1910, and the village was established at that time. The fine old house had been badly neglected, and burned in 1934. Recent Hoxie population was reported as 50 (in 2000), but it is hard to see how that many folks inhabit the area unless a large number of nearby farms is included. The gin was built before 1910.

Hutto Co-op Gins

The gins at Hutto, Texas are a good example of how progress is causing gins to disappear from the landscape. The Hutto Community History implies that at one time Hutto sported up to four gins. The gins shown in the photos below resulted from a farmer's co-op organization in 1938. In July

of 1949 lightening struck about three weeks before harvest, and the resulting fire destroyed the #1 gin. It was quickly rebuilt (the #1 gin is the closest in the photograph) and was back in operation for that year's ginning season. The #2 gin was constructed in 1952 behind the #1 gin. In 1979, 8,200 bales of cotton were ginned from trailers delivered to the gin and in 1992 over 10,000 bales of cotton were ginned from modules delivered to the site.

The last bale of cotton was ginned at approximately eleven a.m. on October 17th, 2001, and the adjacent co-op feed store closed in 2004. The photographs on these pages were taken in June, 2006. By then, the interior of the gin had been gutted, and only the shell remained.

Parts of the gin and co-op were incorporated for a time into a Wag-a-Bag store, which maintained much of the historic character of the buildings. In the summer of 2008, a Farmer's Market was initiated on the site, and the City of Hutto has announced plans to incorporate the gin and nearby grain silos into a new city hall/civic center complex.

"The Largest Cotton Gin in ...."

Texans have never been noted for downplaying their accomplishments, and cotton ginning provides no exception. Below are a few of the claims:

Calvert, TX (est. 1871): "Cotton production was still so important to the area after the Civil War that early in the 1870s, the Gibsons of Galveston transported a story-and-a-half European flywheel on a twenty-oxen cart to Calvert. After a trip that took several months, the Gibsons built the world's largest cotton gin in the town. Until fire destroyed the structure in 1965, Calvert residents lived, worked, ate, and slept to the slow, churning rhythm of steam (and, later, diesel) engines turning the flywheel."
("Calvert, Texas: Preserving a Town's Heritage," Ancestry Magazine, vol. 16 no. 3, May/June 1998.)

"Established in 1876 by P.C. Gibson, the Gibson family operated the oil mill and gin in Calvert. In 1912 it was the largest cotton gin in the world." *(Calvert Historical Foundation)*

"One of Calvert's most interesting features is a gin that was proclaimed the largest in the world and was so featured in the geography books used in Texas schools (and in "Ripley's Believe It or Not"). Colonel J. H. Gibson first built this gin in 1875; at first it had only two stands. Later, it had twenty stands and could gin four bales at once, with a daily output of one hundred and fifty bales. It is now a gin and cotton oil mill and is operated by the descendants of Colonel Gibson." *(History of Calvert Texas)*

"Sprinkled around the park and cemetery, Victorian mansions of rich merchants and cotton-plantation owners remind strollers of a bygone era. Two of the most striking occupy an entire city block each. Built in 1905 and 1906 for brothers P.C. and Jack Gibson, both houses are enhanced with soaring Ionic columns and two-story wraparound porches. The interiors boast extensive wood wainscoting, immense pocket doors and numerous fireplaces.

The Gibson brothers owned the Gibson Gin and Oil Co., once the largest cotton gin in the world. It was destroyed by fire in 1965." *(Roots Web)*

Corsicana: "H. L. Scales who came to Corsicana in the early 1900's from South Texas had the distinction of owning what was at that time the largest cotton gin in the world, located on a switch end of the H. and T. C. Railroad on Collin Street between the Navarro Cotton Oil Mill and the main railroad line." *(The Handbook of Texas On Line.)*

Crosbyton, TX: "…. marketing center for hogs, wheat, and grain sorghum, Crosbyton was also at one time the home of the world's largest cotton gin." *(The Handbook of Texas On Line.)*

Lubbock: Giant new gin gives cotton producers a lift

"Lubbock cotton growers could move their product to market faster than before when the highest-capacity gin in Texas goes online this year. …… The plant could eventually process 120 bales per hour, or more than 2,000 bales a day, according to the release - making the facility the second largest in the world." *(Joshua Hull, Lubbock AVALANCHE-JOURNAL Saturday, October 17, 2009.)*

Martindale, TX: The A.H. Smith cotton gin, built in 1910 and closed in 1944, proclaims it to be "The Largest Cotton Gin in the World for Breeding Seed Exclusively"

Odem, TX: Smith Co-op Gin, Odem — Smith Gin is the largest cotton gin in plant size outside of Australia. ……… present plant was built in 2004.

Sherman, TX: *The Biggest Cotton Gin Burned.* Sherman, Texas, Oct. 23. This evening the cotton gin, four stories high, and the largest gin plant in the world, the property of the Sherman Oil and Cotton Company, was destroyed by fire. The Fire Department prevented the flames from spreading to the oil mills near by. Two hundred and fifty bales of cotton burned in the sheds, and the incandescent electric light plant near the gin is disabled. The city will be in darkness for at least several days. The gin plant was worth over $50,000. The property was well insured. *(The New York Times, Oct. 24, 1891.)*

Tornillo, TX: "....The first large-scale cotton production began in 1918. Growers planted a 600-acre field and set up a two-stand cotton gin. In 1990 cotton was still the main crop, and the largest cotton gin in the state operated at Tornillo. It ginned 90 percent of the cotton grown in the El Paso valley." *(The Handbook of Texas On Line.)*

Johnson City Feed Mill and Gin

Johnson City, at the intersection of SH 290 and SH 281, is of course most famous as the hometown of President Lyndon Baines Johnson. The town site on the Pedernales River was chosen by vote during a barbecue at the ranch of James Polk Johnson in 1879. Land for the town was offered by Johnson, who had settled in the area after service with the Confederacy in the Civil War. He had enlisted in Texas at age 16. James Polk was a nephew of Lyndon B. Johnson's grandfather, Sam Ealy Johnson, Sr.

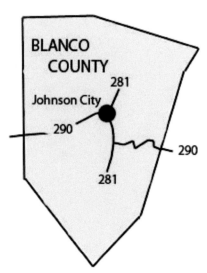

When the town was established and named after him, he changed from rancher to businessman and established a number of businesses and buildings, including a grist mill and steam-powered cotton gin on Town Creek. The mill/gin was built in about 1880. The building was purchased by George Crofts in about 1940, and converted to milling and feed grain production, ending operation as a gin at that time. Crofts designed and built much of the mechanical equipment used in the mill.

The feed mill operated until the late 1970s. It now struggles along with a winery, café, and various antique shops.

The mill is located at 103 W. Main Street (SH 290) in Johnson City.

Jonah Gin

Jonah sports a farm that raises organically produced vegetables and in addition is graced by the shadow of an abandoned gin.

The town submitted various names to establish a post office, but each attempt was turned down by the Post Office Department.

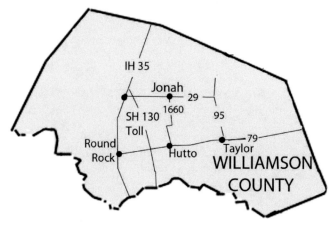

The elders decided the town was a Jonah, and so submitted that name, which was accepted. A town was born! However, the name proved prophetic, and the town suffered a devastating flood in 1921 followed by a fire in 1927 that destroyed the downtown business district.

The *Williamson County Sun* reported that Jonah was hard hit in the 1921 flood (See *Thrall Cooperative Gin*). Every home was inundated. Mr. A. J. Rhodes' restaurant was moved 40 yards and the Christian church was washed across the Milam branch of the San Gabriel River, and each of the other churches in town was damaged.

"Mr. Rhodes, a merchant at Jonah, found a three hundred pound hog in a bed in his house during the flood. Bob Hicks drifted a bale of cotton into the Methodist church at Jonah. It is not known whether Bob will donate the cotton to the church, or whether Mr. Rhodes appropriated the hog."

Kimbro, Lund and New Sweden Gins

The villages of Kimbro, Lund and New Sweden are clustered northeast of Austin in the blacklands farming area. They were founded by Swedish immigrants following the Civil War. Kimbro and Lund have mostly disappeared, although historic schoolhouses have been preserved at Kimbro and nearby Manda, and New Sweden still boasts an active, beautiful and oft-visited Lutheran Church. The descendents of the original settlers still farm much of the land in the region.

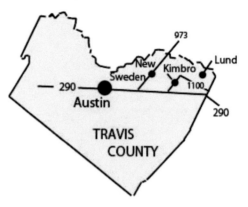

Gin at Kimbro

The Kimbro gin is set well back from FM 1100 near the intersection with Kimbro West Road.

The Lund Gin

This gin is located on Lund-Carlson Road about 12 miles east of New Sweden.

New Sweden Gin

This gin was found by exploring along the aptly named New Sweden Gin Road, northeast of the village of New Sweden. The gin is on the north side of the road. A gin was reported to be operating in New Sweden as early as 1882, but this one appears of more recent vintage, although it might have been built on the original gin site.

It is in complete disrepair, and has partially collapsed and fallen into itself.

Kyle Gin

The International and Great Northern Railroad constructed a railway line between San Antonio and Austin, which after many mergers, foreclosures, reorganizations and purchases, finally became part of the present Union Pacific system. The city is named for Ferg Kyle, who deeded 200 acres to the I&GN to establish the town.

Kyle has become a bedroom community because of its easy access to Austin via Interstate 35, and so land has appreciated considerably in recent years. This combination usually spells doom for abandoned gins in or near a community unless the building can be reused for a contemporary purpose. This is the case for the Kyle gin, which has been converted into a barbeque restaurant.

Cotton Pickin' in Texas

Picking cotton was predominantly a by-hand labor intensive activity until well into the 1940s. The cotton bolls opened at harvest time, but still maintained their horny sharp edges, and cotton pickers experienced bloody hands and aching backs as they stooped to pick cotton and drag heavy-laden sacks along each cotton row. The title of the book *From Can See to Can't* [1997] describes the sunup to sundown work day of cotton farmers and pickers from the slavery period until the early 20th century. Development of a mechanical picker was a clear need, but the peculiar structure of the cotton boll makes extraction of clean cotton a challenge for mechanical picker designers.

Early mechanical pickers could only harvest one row of cotton at a time; they nevertheless could replace up to 40 hand pickers. Modern pickers traverse six to eight rows at once. Two types of mechanical pickers are in common use. The spindle picker removes cotton and seed from the boll with barbed spindles; a series of mechanical operations removes the cotton from the spindles and collects it into a basket for later consolidation into a "module builder" for compaction and transfer to a gin. The second type of harvester is the "stripper" picker. These harvesters strip the entire plant of both open and unopened bolls, along with much plant trash. Some plant matter is separated from the cotton by dropping heavier matter before the lint makes it to the basket at the rear of the picker.

Cotton strippers are used chiefly in Texas, where it is often too windy to grow picker varieties of cotton. Harvesting usually occurs after application of a chemical defoliant or the natural defoliation that occurs after a freeze, and the picking is usually done in a single operation rather than in several passes as the crop matures. This leads to somewhat lower average quality seed, and may be another reason for the demise of seed mills such as in Martindale.

The increasing use of the stripper picker was a factor in the demise of many smaller gins, where owners couldn't afford to upgrade the gin stands to remove the additional bolls and trash in the stripper product. Without the required gin upgrade, the ginned cotton retained trash, and thus sold at a lower market price. As roads were improved and transportation of picked cotton became easier, cotton farmers naturally moved from older local gins to more modern gins that could remove most of the trash, and where they could therefore gain a higher price.

The LaGrange Cotton Press

After picked cotton was ginned, it emerged from the gin with a high ratio of volume to weight; in other words, it was fluffy! It was therefore hard to ship to a cotton mill unless it was compacted in some way. Many large gins incorporated cotton compresses, but these were expensive pieces of equipment, making them uneconomical for smaller gins. Cotton from smaller gins was shipped to a central cotton

compress, which was often located near a rail line so that compressed cotton bales could be centrally stored and shipped.

LaGrange had a central compress facility, including a press built to the Webb patent design. The press went into operation late in the 19th or early 20th century. On February 27, 1906, the press complex burned and the surrounding storage and shipping facilities were lost.

Hand-colored postcard showing the LaGrange compress fire of 1906. The cotton compress is clearly visible amid the flames. (Courtesy Will Beauchamp Collection and Texas Escapes web site: www.texasescapes.com)

The press survived the fire, and a new press complex was built. It operated until 1971, was dismantled in 2006, and the press itself was finally scrapped in 2010 . It was a testament to 19th century engineering.

LaGrange cotton press in 2008

The inventor of this particular style of compress, Samuel J. Webb, was born September 3, 1862 in Homer, Louisiana. After perfecting his design in the 1880s, compress production began in York, Pennsylvania, shifted to the Scott Foundry in Reading, and finally in 1902 to the Webb Press Company in Minden, Louisiana, where Webb made his home.

Samuel Webb and his brother Robert D. Webb filed a series of patents on the steam powered hydraulic press and improvements, the first issuing in June 1899. A patent filed in 1900 and issued in 1906 shows an arrangement nearly identical to the LaGrange press. The press operated by injecting steam into the bottom of the steam cylinder seen on the top of the press. Steam forced the piston upwards, causing cotton loaded in wooden cribs on the ground level platen to be forced upwards and compressed against the upper platen. Steel bands were then strapped around the bales, and the pressed bales were stored for shipping. Most press facilities had large storage buildings for the cotton awaiting pressing and shipment.

Storage building with LaGrange cotton press in the background, 2008.

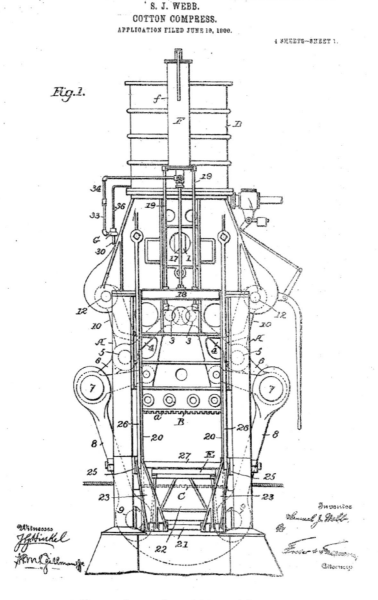

No. 828,002.

PATENTED AUG. 7, 1906.

S. J. WEBB.
COTTON COMPRESS.
APPLICATION FILED JUNE 19, 1900.

4 SHEETS—SHEET 1.

A figure from the 1906 Webb patent.

Other Webb presses of this type are known to exist in New Orleans; Charlotte, North Carolina; and Galveston and Natchitoches, Texas. They are fast disappearing for the same reasons that the gins themselves have disappeared: the shift in production areas for cotton, the increase in the value of land, making them vulnerable to demolition to make way for other uses; and the introduction of better technology. A few remain because they are simply "too big to scrap."

Lexington Gin

The town of Lexington is the oldest settlement in Lee County, sparsely settled in 1830. It became more of a community as part of a land grant issued after the Texas Revolution to James Shaw in 1837. The Civil War took many of the young men from Lexington, but it was repopulated by a group emigrating from Mississippi after the War.

Titus Mundine, a 300 pound politician from Lexington (1826-1872), was originally unpopular in Lee County for strongly opposing secession, but later became well-known for perhaps being the first Texas politician to champion women's suffrage. Lexington thrived for a time after the arrival of the San Antonio and Aransas Pass railroad in 1890, but like many smaller communities, suffered during the Depression years. Now, an annual Chocolate Lovers Festival is held each October, and Lexington is home of Snow's Barbeque, voted in 2008 as "Best in Texas" by *Texas Monthly* and "Best Texas BBQ in the World" by the *New Yorker* magazine.

Lexington's abandoned gin is at the northwest corner of Fourth and Giddings Streets.

Martindale Gins

At one time, the San Marcos River powered a series of mills and gins scattered along its length. Dams along the river diverted water into spillways, and water wheels were geared to power mill and ginning machinery. Martindale was home over the years to a number of gins that overlooked and were powered by the San Marcos, and two that 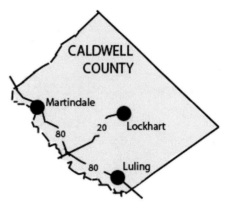 remain show the typical configuration, backing up to the river. One of these is just west of the town center set back from State Highway 80, and appears to have long been abandoned. The floor is rotted and unsafe, and it has collected the usual amount of junk and abandoned equipment. This is probably the gin and corn mill established by W.S. Smith and operated by waterpower from the dam.

The turkey vultures perched atop the building seem content to observe the passing traffic, but do add to the feeling of dereliction. It

seems fruitless to try to imagine the original uses of the abandoned machinery around these combined milling/ginning operations.

Traveling eastward from the W.S. Smith gin and entering the village of Martindale, you encounter the well-preserved brick building originally occupied by the A.H. Smith gin, built in about 1910. Smith replaced an earlier rock and wood dam on the San Marcos with a concrete one, which still graces Martindale with a pleasant pond on the river after more than 100 years.

The Smith gin is a handsome brick structure. The gin closed for business in 1944. It made no bones about being "The Largest Cotton Gin in the World for Planting Seed Exclusively". The backlands prairie around Martindale produced high-grade cotton, and the Smith gin and others nearby were able to sell the ginned cottonseed for planting seed throughout Texas.

With the closing of the gins, Martindale has undergone a slow decline in population and a loss of local businesses. It is still a handsome town that maintains an aura of its more prosperous past. Moviemakers have chosen it as a period set for *The Newton Boys, A Perfect World*, and *The Texas Chainsaw Massacre.* It is difficult to separate buildings reflecting Martindale's past from those that were modified for movie sets. Hopes for revitalizing the downtown are strong.

The Maxwell Gin

Maxwell sits just north of Texas Route 142 where County Road 241 (Railroad Street) crosses the Union Pacific tracks. The Maxwell gin has been converted into a popular music venue that caters to parties, weddings, and live music shows.

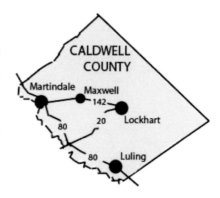

Niederwald Planter's Gin

Niederwald lies on SH 21 at the T- junction with westbound FM 2001. The name means "low woods" in German, and was supposedly named for the low-growing mesquite trees in the area.

The gin, on the north side of SH 21 just west of the T, is heavily overgrown with weeds. It was clearly a very large operation in its prime, with multiple buildings, now all falling into sad disrepair.

The gin combined with the nearby Mendoza gin, and operated as the Niederwald-Mendoza gin from 1913 until the 1970s.

A stately Fairbanks-Morse model Y, 2-cylinder 100 hp, 300 rpm semi-diesel engine that once powered the gin remains in the building. These engines entered the market after the expiration of Rudolph Diesel's patent in 1912, but were not true diesel engines. They use a hot chamber to ignite the fuel/air mixture after relatively low compression, rather than the self-ignition at the high temperatures caused by the very high compression in a true diesel engine. An identical engine of 1924 vintage has been restored by the Tri-State Gas Engine & Tractor Association, Inc. of Portland, Indiana.

Pflugerville

Henry Pfluger settled 160 acres of farmland near Austin in 1849, later moving to a larger farm near the present town of Pflugerville in 1853. The Missouri-Kansas-Texas (Katy) railroad arrived in 1904, initiating growth of the village, and two gins were established, one by Henry's son Otto (some sources say sons George and William) in 1904 and a second in

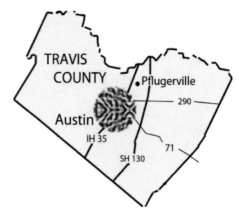

1909. Black workers in the cotton industry were not allowed to live in town, and settled in the Colored Addition, where lots were available for $50.

The 1904 Pfluger gin burned in 1931, and was replaced on the same site on Pecan Street. There have been rumors of ghost activity in the basement of the new gin. The First United Methodist Church bought the land in 2006, and constructed an education building nearby in 2009.

Redwood Gin

Old Gin Road forms an S curve through the old section of Redwood. The gin itself appears to have been converted into a residence with spacious grounds and gardens.

Redwood has other interesting abandoned structures, including an auto repair shop.

Rice's Crossing Gin

The gin at Rice's Crossing was in operation until about 2009, and is now apparently another victim of decreasing local cotton production. The gin is on FM 973 just north of the intersection with FM 1660 in Williamson County, barely north of the Travis County line.

Rice's Crossing was settled in 1845 under the name of Blue Hill, and was granted a post office in 1849, the second one in Williamson County. James O. Rice had served with distinction in the Texas War of Independence, as a Texas Ranger, and in the Mexican War, and was given large land grants in the area for his service. He is particularly remembered for his defeat of Manuel Flores at the Battle on the San Gabriels in 1839 in the Texas-Indian Wars. He was postmaster during the original Blue Hill post office period of 1849-1857. After the post office was closed and then re-established in 1872, the old name of Blue Hill was changed to Rice and then Rice's Crossing in his honor.

San Marcos Farmers Union Gin

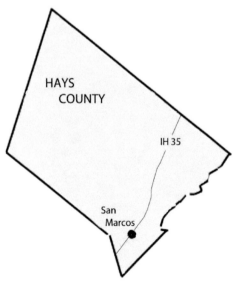

The Farmers Union Gin replaced an earlier wood-framed gin that burned. It is located on Grove Street, just south of Guadalupe Street, in San Marcos. According to Troy Miller, who operates *Texas Reds*, the restaurant that has occupied the building since 1991, construction started on the "fireproofed" new building in 1908, and it opened for business in 1911. The gin operated until 1966. The building was declared a Texas Historic Landmark in 1977.

Sharp Gin

Sharp is located on FM 487 just north of Thorndale in Milam County. The first gin opened in 1896.

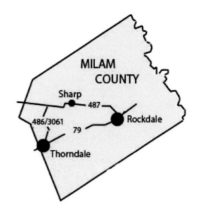

Sims, Mudville, and Mooring

The towns of Sims, Mudville, and Mooring lie close together on FM 50 just north of its intersection with SH 21 in Brazos County. The towns all grew with the coming of the Texas and New Orleans railroad (which became part of the Southern Pacific and now the Union Pacific) and the parallel Hearne and Brazos Valley railroad. A T&NO station was established in Sims, and an H&BV station in Mudville (supposedly named after its most abundant resource and, sadly, no connection with *Casey at the Bat*). The H&BV became part of the Houston and Texas Central in 1914, which in turn also became part of the Southern Pacific, which was acquired by the Union Pacific. Thus, the two parallel tracks passing through Sims, Mudville and Mooring are each now part of the Union Pacific. There is an operating gin alongside the tracks in Mooring, but the shell of the abandoned gin shown above lies across FM 50 to the east.

A diesel engine appears to be the only item salvaged from the gin machinery, and it sits awaiting restoration.

Sisterdale Gin

Sisterdale was founded by German settlers escaping from the aborted 1848 revolution in Germany. It was one of five German colonies founded by a group of intellectuals known as the *Latiners* because of their belief that knowledge of Latin was a prerequisite to higher learning, and was therefore a sign of intellectual attainment.

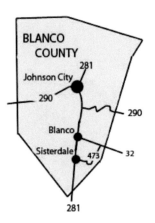

The fine old Sisterdale gin building was built in 1885, and now houses the Sister Creek Winery; an excellent way to preserve a mark of the gin heritage.

Sommer Family Gin

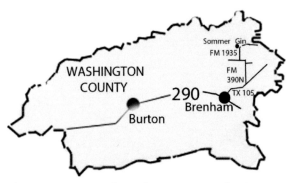

The Sommer family operated gins on their family farm from the mid-1800s until the final closure in 1982. The gins began with mule and horse power, switched to a new location with steam power in 1885, moved to a new and final location in 1921 still using steam power fired by cordwood, switched to oil fuel in 1936, switched again to butane fuel in 1940, and made the final conversion to electric power in 1952.

The gin is complete with all equipment in its state as of closing. It was operating three 80-saw gin stands that fed a lint cleaner and two hydraulic bale presses.

Gin stands

Lint Cleaner

Bale Press

The gin finally closed in 1982 due to the increased trash in "picker" cotton that the older gin stands could not completely clean, coupled with electric rate changes imposed by the Bluebonnet Electrical Co-op, which had originally given "per bale ginned" rates. The Co-op found that it couldn't profitably provide year-around commercial (240 VAC) electrical service that was only used a few months of the year, and raised rates to a level that made the ginning operation itself unprofitable.

The gin sits on a site overlooking the Brazos River.

Staples Gin

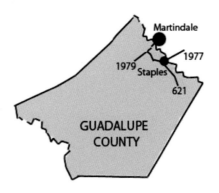

The first water-powered gin at Staples was built on the present site alongside the San Marcos River (at what is now the low-water bridge across the San Marcos carrying FM 1977) by Leonidas Hardeman in 1867. This was apparently prior to his interest in what became Zedler's Mill downstream on the San Marcos in Luling. In 1895, a dynamo powered by the San Marcos was added that provided lighting to the mill.

View of the gin pond behind the dam looking downstream, taken from the low-water bridge.

In the early 1900s, the gin was converted partially to steam so that operations could continue in times of low water. A larger dynamo was added in 1903 to provide electricity to the growing village of Staples. The gin passed through many owners until the formation of the Staples Farmer's Co-op in 1951.

Over the life of the gin, other operations, including grain milling and cane crushing, were added. A grain storage building and office complex were added in 1966.

The gin operated into the 1970's, and is now a private home.

The village of Staples itself finally bowed to progress and after proudly standing on its own for over 150 years, incorporated in May, 2008.

Cotton Control- Monopolies and Restraints

The number of cotton gins in the US peaked at nearly 31,000 in 1902, leading to the organization of state and national ginners associations to further their economic and political issues. (By 2008, only 734 operating gins remained, according to the National Cotton Ginners Association.) The introduction of technical advances and sudden innovations in ginning and presses affected cotton production in Texas and elsewhere. Many of the attempts to introduce and control new technologies led to extended legal battles, and, indeed, some of the old fights have emerged anew because of contemporary innovations and conditions.

Gin, Compress and Oil Mill Monopolies

Monopolies have been a part of cotton ginning since Eli Whitney attempted to keep a monopoly on all gins. He tried to control use of his technology through vigorously pursuing patent infringement suits against anyone who used his gin invention without his permission. Piracy was so widespread that he went bankrupt in the attempt, and gin manufacturers proliferated quickly.

Farmers generally liked to sell their seed where they had their cotton ginned so that they did not have to handle it further. A battle arose when cottonseed oil mill owners realized that they could gain an advantage by owning their own gins. They thus had direct access to cottonseed. In fact, they could gin cotton at well below the cost of independent gins, and make their profit on the seed that was generated. This, of course, brought considerable displeasure to the independent ginners, who brought suit to prevent this vertical integration which was driving many of them out of business. A Mississippi case went all the way to the US Supreme Court, which found in 1921, in agreement with lower courts in the State of Mississippi, that oil mills could not use their monopolistic powers in this way, and must divest themselves of all gins not immediately adjacent to the oil mills.

A contemporary fight on cottonseed is being played out because of the introduction of genetically modified (GM) cotton. This cotton resists herbicides, so that an herbicide can be used in cotton fields to control weeds without injuring the cotton, and per acre production is greatly increased. A single producer, Monsanto, controlled over 80 percent of the GM seed market in 2010, and controls seed distribution by requiring that no seed ginned from their GM cotton be retained by the farmer for replanting. Farmers believe this to be unfair, as the seed is a product of their work and its loss is a considerable economic penalty. Monsanto has brought suit against a number of farmers who have retained seed, and suits on the question of whether the system constitutes a monopoly are working through the judicial system. The question may become moot, as other seed producers are developing rival GM products.

The Round Bale Battle

Cotton presses were traditionally of the type shown under the LaGrange Cotton Press entry, and resulted in rectangular (called "square") bales. These had certain disadvantages; they were difficult to wrap and strap, and tended to develop holes in the burlap wrapping that often resulted in soiled or wet cotton being delivered to the customer. The wrapping and strapping added about 23 pounds to the weight of a 500 pound square bale. The holes in the burlap wrapping resulted from rough handling, but also because samples of the cotton might be pulled from the bale at many points along its travel from press to final customer.

In the late 1800s, two patents were issued for round bale cotton presses. The George A. Lowry patent was for a system of rotating lint winding onto a mandrel with steam-powered platens at each end of the round bale to provide compression, and final baling of the roll. The William T. Bessonette patent was for a carpet-rolled bale with two diametrically opposed steam roller presses that compressed the cotton layers into sheets and then onto the roll during the rolling process, and no baling was required to maintain the final roll.

The 1895 *Atlanta Cotton States and International Exposition* featured an opening day speech by President Grover Cleveland, a large Ferris wheel, display of the Liberty Bell, John Philip Sousa and his band playing the new march "King Cotton", the introduction of the screened moving picture, and Buffalo Bill Cody's Wild West Show, but is most remembered for the "Atlanta Compromise" speech on race relations by Booker T. Washington. Of importance for this book was the unveiling of a round-bale cotton press by predecessors of the American Cotton Company, using the Bessonette patent. The round bale had a higher density (32 pounds of ginned cotton per cubic foot compared with 25 for square bales).

The American Cotton Company, and its chief competitor, the Planters Compress Company using the Lowry patent, began to lease round bale presses. This innovation began to take hold, and the number of round bales produced rose from about 500,000 in 1899 to a peak of 980,000 in 1902. This was still a small fraction of the total bales produced, which exceeded 10,000,000. By 1908, the American Cotton Company owned outright about 100 gins, and directly controlled presses at 200 more through press lease agreements. The question of whether American Cotton was a trust entered the presidential campaign of 1900, with Teddy Roosevelt railing against the company.

The round bale companies fought hard to spread the use of their press, but were resisted strongly by the entrenched square-bale press owners. The round-balers fought for and won decreased insurance rates, arguing that losses due to fire and water damage were smaller for round bales, and they negotiated lower shipping rates with steamship companies due to the higher density, meaning more cotton could be shipped in a single hull. They also attempted to get decreased per bale and per carload rail shipping rates (and thus gain a competitive advantage over square bale presses), but were rebuffed by both the Texas Railroad Commission and the Interstate Commerce Commission in 1915.

The Texas Cotton Ginners Association, originally founded in Waco in 1897 to promote the interests of gin owners, became embroiled in the fight between square bale and round bale ginners and presses, and disbanded over the fight in 1901. A gathering of ginners in 1909 met to reorganize, and the present TCGA was finally chartered in 1929.

The square bale press operators were successful in resisting round bale presses, and round bale production rapidly declined until, in 1913, production was under 100,000 bales. The Planters Compress Company had been dissolved some years earlier by court order.

On January 15, 1915, the *New York Times* reported that the American Round Bale Press Company, the successor to the American Cotton Company, had declared bankruptcy, citing the cutoff of European markets due to World War I, and the fact that of 59 presses owned by the company, only one Texas and one Oklahoma round bale press remained in operation. This appeared to end the round bale battle.

But wait! In 2007, John Deere introduced a round-baling cotton picker, which has reopened the issue. The system picks cotton and produces a round bale of seed cotton, ready -wrapped for transport to the gin. The baling machinery appears to be similar in concept to the Bessonett machine.

The John Deere 7760 Cotton Picker/Baler
(Courtesy, Alex Bruggemann, Dalby, Australia)

Gins must now handle round, cubical and rectangular modules for feeding into the gins, depending on the type of picker/module builder used.

Transport and Holdup Point Monopolies

The complex system of picking, ginning, pressing, and transporting cotton to spinning and weaving mills provided opportunities for entrepreneurs, monopolists, and con men to prosper. When what are now styled as "holdup points" were identified and obtained by enterprising merchants, it was possible to gain great leverage over prices.

A prime example was the Port of New Orleans, which was the main transshipment port for cotton from the southern gins to both the mills of the US north and England in the late 19th century and beyond. At that time, most baled cotton was shipped by riverboat to New Orleans, unloaded and stored in warehouses, and then reloaded on outbound ships. Because few alternatives existed, the costs of transshipment had to be added to the final price of cotton. The New Orleans longshoremen's union as well as warehouse owners were free to charge almost any rate as long as no other shipment option was available. The coming of the railroads provided an alternative in two ways; first, they eliminated the step of unloading from the riverboats, which was more easily handled from freight cars; and second, it became possible to use the railroads to ship to other outbound ports rather than relying on Mississippi riverboat traffic, reducing or eliminating the New Orleans advantage.

Interior of a Southern Cotton Press by Night, Harper's Weekly, March 24, 1883.
(Courtesy, 19th & Early 20th Century Labor Prints, 1863-1908, Southern Labor Archives, Special Collections Department, Georgia State University Library)

A similar holdup point was at the Port of Galveston, where most Texas cotton was transshipped. The Galveston Wharf and Cotton Press Company was formed in 1854 to consolidate various private firms. It controlled transshipment and pressing prices, and was known locally as "The Octopus of the Gulf." Late in the 19th century, collusion between the two major coastal shipping lines that served the port also eliminated competition in shipping rates. Resulting shipment prices to cotton brokers were thus set to whatever level could be imposed before brokers sought other less convenient but cheaper ports where lower shipping costs were set by competition. Despite the high costs resulting from the monopolies, by 1900 Galveston was the largest cotton shipping port in the world. The combination of the disastrous 1900 hurricane and the later opening of the Houston Ship Channel ended Galveston's dominance, and the wharves came under control of the Texas Railroad Commission in 1911.

Theon Gin

I viewed the gin at Theon in January, 2011. While photographing the gin exterior, I was hailed by Mr. Jim Built, the owner of the gin. I explained what I was doing, and he graciously provided me with a tour of the gin interior. He noted that the gin was 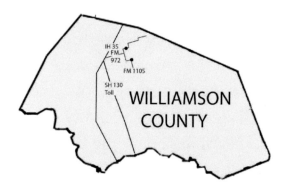 built in 1883, and ginned cotton every year until 1993, when about 300 bales were ginned. It was too expensive to comply at that time with new EPA pollution standards, and the gin was closed.

The gin originally was wood-sided, but the siding was replaced with corrugated tin in the 1950s. The gin operated on steam until about 1959, when it converted to two diesel engines, one to operate the blowers, and the other to operate the gin stands. Most of the original equipment is in the gin, including many of the original wooden pulleys and belt wheels.

The belts have been pulled off the pulleys to prevent stretching, as was always done at the end of each ginning season.

The hydraulic bale presses are on a rotary table, allowing cotton to make one bale to be loaded and pressed while the previous bale is removed. The press positions are then traded.

The gin stands take raw cotton from the fields, and remove the seed. The seed is removed to the seed bin for sale to a seed mill, or returned to the farmer for planting next year's crop.

There is some talk of restarting the gin for at least a one-day demonstration.

The truck under the seed bin is a '46 chevy, bought new and operated until the gin closed.

The firetruck was not originally part of the gin, but is the property of Mr. Built, an avid collector and restorer.

Thorndale Gin

Thorndale was established in 1878, about three miles west of its

present site. Like many Texas towns, it carried out a short move after the International - Great Northern Railroad was built through the nearby area. The town was named by a railroad employee to reflect the thorny vegetation (mesquite, thorn, prickly pear, and sagebrush) rife in the region. Thorndale incorporated in 1929 with a reported population of 1,500, just in time for the onset of the Great Depression. The number of residents fell to about 1,000 by 1931, and it had fallen to 851 by 1952. A nearby aluminum plant and associated lignite fueled electrical generating station have provided employment in recent years.

The Quonset hut shown above was in operation when photographed in July of 2006. On a return in 2010, it was gone, along with the pickup truck, but the old portion of the gin remained.

Thrall Co-Operative Gin

Thrall straddles SH 79 at the intersection with County Road 424, about 35 miles northeast of Austin. Thrall is famous for receiving the greatest rainfall ever recorded in the United States in a 24 hour period; 38.2 inches ending at 7 am on September 10,

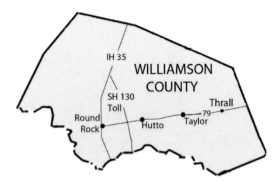

1921. The rain was a result of the stalled remnants of a hurricane that came ashore near Vera Cruz, Mexico and turned north. The resulting flood caused 215 deaths statewide, the deadliest in Texas history. In Taylor, about seven miles east of Thrall, 87 people were lost.

The city is named for Homer Spellman Thrall, a Methodist minister and historian who wrote five books, including the much admired *A Pictorial History of Texas, from the Earliest Visits of European Adventurers, to A.D. 1883*.

The Thrall gin, built in 1965 to replace an older gin that was torn down a year later, is the only commercially operating gin shown in this book. The history of the town melds so well with the surrounding towns and their lost gins that it seems appropriate to include it. Along with the gins in Granger, Taylor and Waterloo, it is one of the four operating gins left in Williamson County of the more than 40 that thrived in the early 1940s.

Walburg Gin

Walburg, on FM 972 is northeast of Austin in Williamson County and reported a population of 250 in 2000. The Walburg gin has been converted into a restaurant, biergarten and entertainment venue.

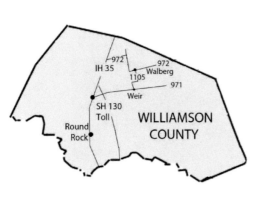

Winchester

Winchester, like many Texas cotton farming communities, has seen a boom-and-bust cycle. During the cotton boom, the village grew to 18 businesses in 1900, and was served by two railroads. A gin was in operation at least as early as 1902. As cotton declined, the population dropped to 220 in 1950, and in the 1980s the population was 50, and four businesses remained. The population remained at about 50 in 2000.

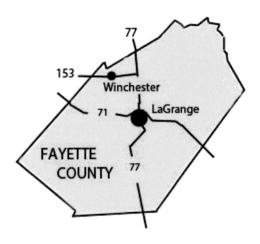

Old Woodswitch Gin

Woodswitch Gin Road crosses FM 50 about four miles north of Mumford. The newer (and still operating) Woodswitch Gin is to the West of FM 50 at the Union Pacific tracks, while the abandoned Old Woodswitch Gin lies to the east on a rutted oil field and farm access road, and is nearly covered with overgrowth.

The closest town to the gin is Mumford, which retains its post office but little else. It was established when Jesse Mumford began a ferry across the nearby Brazos in 1855. An iron bridge replaced the ferry in 1895, but the bridge and most of Mumford was washed away by a flood in 1899.

Zedler's Mill and Gin, Luling

One of the most well-known and oft-visited abandoned gins in Central Texas is located Northwest of where State Highway 80 crosses the San Marcos river in Luling.

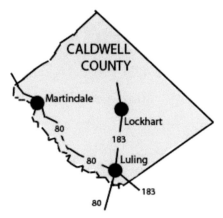

The Handbook of Texas History notes that Fritz Zedler was born in Friedberg, Prussia, on March 23, 1840. His family moved to Texas in 1852, landing at Indianola. He held several jobs and began small businesses, and served briefly in the Civil War. In 1862 he obtained a release from military service and married Louise Fechner of Yorktown. They parented eleven children. In 1872 the family moved to Sandies in Gonzales County, where Zedler established a mill complex. He moved to a site near Luling in 1880. The local mill had been built by Leonidas Hardeman (see Staples Gin), James Merriweather, and his older brother, John Merriweather, and used a water wheel on the San Marcos as the power source. Bob Innes, John Orchard, J.K. Walker, and Fritz Zedler purchased the mill sometime between 1883 and 1888. Because of his experience, Zedler operated the mill, and later added a sawmill to the gin and grist mill. He bought out his partners in early 1888.

The oft-repeated gin fate came to bear, and the mill and gin burned on October 15, 1888, but Zedler's customers held their raw cotton until he was able to rebuild. Zedler contracted in 1890 to furnish water from the mill pond to the city of Luling. He left his sons to run the Luling mill from 1891 to 1895 and went to Cuero to manage the mill there. In his absence his sons installed an electric plant at the mill and began supplying power for Luling. Zedler retired in March 1902 and died on September 16, 1932 at age 92. The Zedler home, built in 1900, was restored in 1972. The house and the Zedler mill each received historical markers in 1974.

While photographing Zedler's Mills on Dec. 28, 2006, I met a gentleman who was walking his dog. He said he could remember when the mill was still in operation. He told me about the Zedler family, noting that Zedler himself never left the mill property after his return to Luling, but had a barber chair installed in his home, and had a barber come out from town to provide shaves and haircuts. Two of his daughters lived in the old (restored) house across the road; neither ever married.

He told me that the row of structures to the right of the mill entrance road once housed donkeys and oxen that were used to move baled cotton.

Mule and oxen barn

The City of Luling, through a grant from the National Park Service, has restored the Zedler home, and has long-term plans to develop the mill and gin property into a park and possibly to refurbish the barns into an artist colony and to restore the mill and gin equipment as a historic site.

The rear of Zedler's Mill, showing the millrace and some of the remaining gears originally used to drive the mill and gin, and probably the electrical generator.

Afterword

I have found over forty-five abandoned gin buildings in Central Texas. Over the four-to-five year period of gathering the photographs, active gins have gone out of business (Rice's Crossing), abandoned gins continue to be bulldozed (Fredericksburg) and cotton presses are scrapped (LaGrange). References to long-gone gins abound in the histories of Central Texas towns and villages, but in many cases the towns have disappeared along with the gins. Abandoned gins in smaller towns may last for a considerable time as they join other abandoned structures in the decaying environs and there is no economic need for their razing. Other gins survive through conversion to other uses as in Beyersville (truck repair), Kyle (barbeque restaurant), Sisterdale (winery), San Marcos (steakhouse), Walburg and Maxwell (restaurant and entertainment venues), and others. Some communities continue working to save the gins for community use, as in Belton, Hutto, and Luling, but each of these efforts has been long, and at the time of this writing, fruitless. The gin and museum at Burton and the annual Cotton Gin Festival have gone a long way toward preserving an important part of the past, and it's hoped that this book will help preserve a little more of an important part of Central Texas history.

Acknowledgements

The author thanks all of those who helped in finding information about the gins shown in these pages. Many people responded to e-mail and phone inquiries with useful history, anecdotes, leads to others who might have information, and publications and other sources of information. I will probably miss some who were helpful, as this effort spanned a number of years and went from a hobby to a wish to share the information in the present form. Of particular help have been the websites maintained by the various County, City, and Association historical groups, who have kept priceless information from being lost.

Individual contributors of information about and leads to abandoned gins include Ralph Bachmeyer, owner of the Thrall gin; Will Beauchamp, avid collector of memorabilia on early Texas, including postcards; Gilbert Bohuslav, son of the last owner and operator of the Ammannsville Gin; Jim Built, owner of the Theon gin; Mike Fowler, former Mayor of Hutto and activist in preserving the Hutto Gin and Co-op; Daniel R. Heideman, Mayor, Uhland, Texas; Jody Krankel, Jim Lutz, Marilyn Samuelson, all three active in the Blackland Prairie Concerned Citizens Association; Annamarie Krieg Kolodziej, Richardson, Texas; Troy Miller, co-owner/operator of *Texas Reds*, San Marcos; Sheila Pausewang, City Secretary, Thrall, Texas; Linda Russell, Director, Texas Cotton Gin Museum in Burton, Texas; Wayne Ware, webmaster, Williamson County Historical Commission; and Jeff Youngblood, Arlington, Texas.

Partial List of Sources

Bennett, Charles A.: "Cotton Ginning Systems in the United States and Auxiliary Developments," *The Cotton Ginners' Journal and the Cotton Gin and Oil Mill Press*, Dallas, 1962.

"Continental Eagle Corporation History, 177 Years 1832-2007," Landmarks Foundation of Montgomery, Alabama, 2010.

"Cotton Bale Fire Tests," *The Insurance Press-Fire Insurance*, vol. 15, pg. 4, Aug. 27, 1902.

"Cotton Rates Decision," *Traffic World*, vol. XV, no. 2, pp. 88- 9, 1915.

Ellis, L. Tuffly: "The Round Bale Cotton Controversy," *The Southwestern Historical Quarterly*, Vol. 71, No. 2, pp. 194-225, Oct. 1967.

Fowler, Mike, former Mayor of Hutto, personal communication.

Hainze, Michelle Sharon Gayle Gluck: An Analysis of Cotton Gin Buildings in the South Plains Region, MS Thesis, *Texas Tech University College of Architecture,* August, 1999.

Holmes, Thomas J. and James A. Schmitz, Jr.: "Competition at Work: Railroads vs. Monopoly in the U.S. Shipping Industry," *Federal Reserve Bank of Minneapolis Quarterly Review,* Vol. 25, No. 2, pp. 3–29, Spring, 1967.

Kimmel, Jim: *The San Marcos; A River's Story,* Texas A&M University Press, College Station, 2006.

Lotto, Frank: *Fayette County, Her History and Her People,* Published by the Author through the Sticker Steam Press, Schulenburg, TX. 1902.

Mangialardi, Jr., Gino J., and Anthony, W. Stanley: "Retrospective View of Cotton Gin Dryers," The National Cotton Ginners Association, Memphis, undated (c. 2002).

Mangialardi, Jr., Gino J., and Anthony, W. Stanley: "Cotton Gin Saw Developments," The National Cotton Ginners Association, Memphis, undated (c. 2002).

Mangialardi, Jr., Gino J., and Anthony, W. Stanley: "Bale Presses at Gins, 1960 – 2004," National Cotton Ginners Association, Memphis, undated (c. 2005).

"Report of the US Industrial Commission on Agriculture and Agricultural Labor Including Testimony with Review and Topical Digest Thereof," Vol. X, Washington, D.C., Government Printing Office, 1910.

Sitton, Thad and Dan K. Utley: *From Can See to Can't: Texas Cotton Farmers on the Southern Prairies*, University of Texas Press, Austin, 1997.

Thrall, Homer S.: *A Pictorial History of Texas, from the Earliest Visits of European Adventurers, to A.D. 1883,* N.D. Thomson & Co., St. Louis, 1883.

"1866-1989 Texas Historical Crops Statistics," *Texas Agricultural Statistics Service*, Bulletin 248, August, 1991.

"The St. Louis Board of Fire Underwriters Has Made a Test…," *The Weekly Underwriter*, vol. 56, no. 6, pg 88, Jan. 2-June 26, 1897.

Web Sites of Interest

The James Polk Johnson Cemetery,
http://www.cemeteries-of-tx.com/Wtx/Blanco/cemetery/JOHNSON.htm

History and Background, Texas Boll Weevil Eradication Program,
http://www.txbollweevil.org/Program_information/History.htm

Handbook of Texas On Line (Gives thumbnail sketches of the towns and cities throughout Texas, including those in this book): http://www.tshaonline.org/handbook/online/

Hefner, James: "Too big to scrap - steam cotton compresses," *Railway Preservation News*,
http://server.rypn.org/forums/

Hoxie, John R.: http://genealogytrails.com/ill/cook/chicagobios.htm

www.hutto-heritage-
foundation.org/HISTORY_OF_THE_HUTTO_TEXAS_COMMUNITY.htm

Lummus Corporation history, http://www.lummus.com/history.html

Murphy, Mark and Noe Torres: "UFO Crash in North Texas 1891," *UFO Digest*, April 15, 2008, http://www.ufodigest.com/news/0408/north-texas.html

"Aurora, Texas is Home of the Space Alien Cemetery,"
GoRV Texas, http://gorvtexas.com/aurora.htm

Index

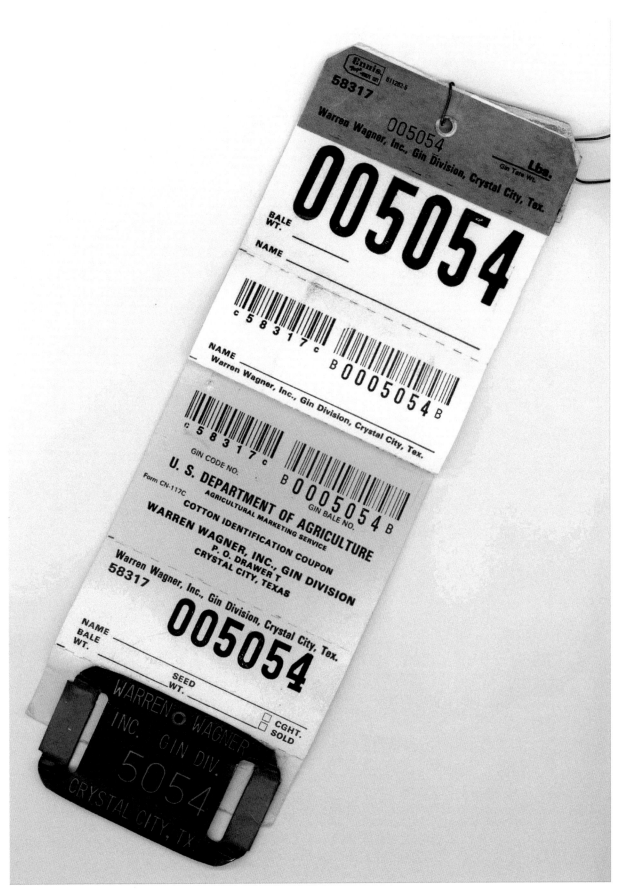

Made in the USA
Coppell, TX
02 November 2021